Laura Ingalls Wilder and the Family Journey

Photos and Graphics by
George Hawkins

Written by
Barb Hawkins

Little House Site Tours LLC
2430 Marlette Rd, Applegate, MI 48401
lhsitetours@email.com
www.lhsitetours.homestead.com

ISBN 978-0-9765951-2-0

Published by
Barbara Hawkins
Little House Site Tours LLC
www.lhsitetours.homestead.com

Introduction

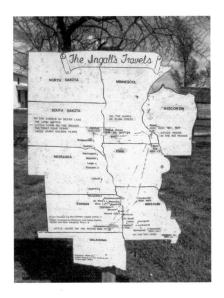

During the summer of 2004, I took a picture of this sign at the Little House Site near Independence, Kansas. The picture was used in my first book, *100 Verses About Laura Ingalls Wilder.*

Later that summer, I purchased a map at one of the Little House Gift Shops showing the travels of the Ingalls and Wilders. Every time I looked at these maps I became more interested in Laura's journeys. The one that fascinated me the most was from De Smet, South Dakota, to Mansfield, Missouri. What was on that route in 1894 that might still be there today? What had been added that would be "beyond Laura's dreams?"

Travel routes have changed and it is difficult to know the exact route the Wilders followed. With this in mind, my husband and I used the maps mentioned above and ventured many times on the journey from De Smet, South Dakota, to Mansfield, Missouri. We found things that 1894 travelers, including the Wilders, might have seen and interesting features that have been added during the past century.

We hope you enjoy our adventures and that you will have the opportunity to travel the route of

Laura Ingalls Wilder and the Family Journey

Thank you to Cheryl Palmlund, Director, LIW Society, De Smet, SD, and Kathy Short, Director, Mansfield Historical Society, Mansfield, MO, for their help with historical photos.

We also want to thank the many directors and volunteers at museums and historical societies in the midwest for their time and wonderful cooperation in sharing facts and pictures.

Barb and George Hawkins
Little House Site Tours

CONTENTS

CONTENTS

Laura and Almanzo 1885 - 1894

Kingsbury County Independent   *July 20, 1894*

> be taken back to Wisconsin for burial.
>
> Manly Wilder started for Missouri last Monday, and will make the trip by team in company with Mr. Cooley. Mr. Wilder has been a resident of De Smet for several years, and is one of those men whom we dislike to see move away.
>
> The horse power

Why would Almanzo (Manly) Wilder move to Missouri? What had happened in De Smet? Why would Almanzo and Laura decide to take their daughter, Rose, and head for the "Land of the Big Red Apple?" Let's look back on their lives together.

From Happy Times to Sad Times

It was August 25, 1885, Almanzo Wilder drove to the Ingalls claim, helped Laura into his buggy, and together they headed to Reverend Brown's home on a hill to the west. This announcement appeared in the
De Smet News Leader   August 29, 1885

> MARRIED.
> WILDER—INGALLS.—At the residence of the officiating clergyman, Rev. E. Brown, August 25, 1885. Mr. Almanzo J. Wilder and Miss Laura Ingalls, both of De Smet.
>
> Thus two more of our respected young people have united in the journey of life. May their voyage be pleasant their joys be many and their sorrows few.

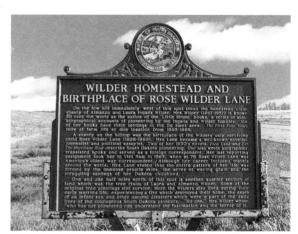

Almanzo had built a small home on his claim north of De Smet. They settled here after their wedding.

Laura and Almanzo   Winter, 1885   After their wedding in De Smet, SD

The next year (December 5, 1886) their daughter, Rose, was born. They were sharing so many happy times in their life together. However, the happy times became saddened the next year when they faced this tragedy.

De Smet Leader, July 30, 1887

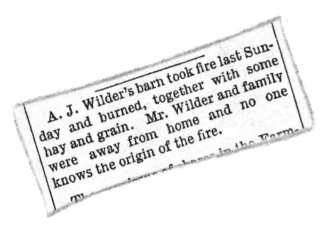

A. J. Wilder's barn took fire last Sunday and burned, together with some hay and grain. Mr. Wilder and family were away from home and no one knows the origin of the fire.

The year, 1887, was a difficult one. After losing their barn to a fire, Laura and Almanzo became ill with diphtheria. Their daughter, Rose, spent a lot of time with her grandparents, Charles and Caroline Ingalls.

Pa Ingalls built this home in town in 1887. It was the final home for the Ingalls. He started by building three rooms and added the rest of the house one room at a time. The house was completed in 1889 and is a favorite stop today for visitors to De Smet.

The Laura Ingalls Wilder Memorial Society, Inc. purchased this home in 1972. It is open for tours and is enjoyed every year by people from all over the world. It is still at its same location on Third Street.

One can see the original cupboards built by Pa Ingalls. The upstairs of the home is open and has furniture used by their daughter, Rose. These items were brought to De Smet after Rose's death. She passed away in 1968 in Connecticut.

It was in the living room of this home that Grace Ingalls married Nathan Dow on October 16, 1901. They settled on his farm near Manchester, just west of De Smet.

For more information about touring this home, contact the Laura Ingalls Wilder Memorial Society in De Smet, South Dakota.

Living in Spring Valley, Minnesota

From Happy Times to Sad Times - Again

Laura and Almanzo spent the winter of 1887-1888 recuperating from diphtheria. It was a difficult time and Almanzo was left with some lifetime health problems.

Kingsbury County News - March 9, 1888

—Mr. and Mrs. Manly Wilder are doing nicely under the care of Dr. Cushman. Are up and around.
— Michael Roberts will herd cattle on

Their daughter, Rose, was 2 1/2 when Laura and Almanzo had a son.

De Smet Leader - July 13, 1889

Dr. Hunter reports the arrival of a 10-pound boy at A. J. Wilder's on Thursday night.

De Smet Leader - August 10, 1889

Mr. and Mrs. A. J. Wilder's little child died Wednesday evening.

Their baby son (unnamed) became the first of the Ingalls and Wilder families to be buried at the De Smet Cemetery.

The year 1889 found the Wilders facing another misfortune when their home burned to the ground. Little was saved.

In the spring of 1890, Laura, Almanzo, and Rose, now just 3 1/2 years old, left De Smet and spent a year with Almanzo's parents on their farm in Spring Valley, MN. They needed a year of rest and the large Wilder farm home provided this for them.

Wilder Farm Home in Spring Valley, Minnesota
torn down in 1926

The Wilders Recuperate for a year in Spring Valley, Minnesota 1890 - 1891

Laura, Almanzo, and Rose attended this church while living with Almanzo's parents in Spring Valley.

Almanzo's parents, James and Angeline Wilder, were supportive members of the church when construction began in 1876. They attended the first church service on Christmas Eve, 1876. The church was completed and dedicated on August 16, 1878.

Today, this church is a museum, operated by the Spring Valley Historical Society. It is a Laura Ingalls Wilder Site and is visited every year by people from all over the world. The fire wagon (at left) is one of the many items on display and was used when the Wilders were living here.

1891 - Laura and Almanzo Look for a Better Place to Live

In 1891, they took a train to Westville, Florida, hoping to find a better climate for their health - especially Almanzo's. In 1892, they moved back to De Smet and again enjoyed the security of friends and family.

Almanzo and Laura bought a small home just a block from the Ingalls home. Laura went to work as a seamstress for a dressmaker and earned a dollar a day. She saved and was able to set aside $100. Almanzo took on various jobs.

Their daughter, Rose, spent a lot of time at the Ingalls home with her grandparents. Her Aunt Mary was blind and was also living at the Ingalls home during this time. Carrie was working at the De Smet newspaper office and Grace was still in school.

Early De Smet and the Buildings Today

On the left is an early picture of the northwest corner of Second Street and Calumet Avenue. This was the location of Pa's office building and stable.

Edward Couse purchased the building and lot from Charles Ingalls and it became Couse Hardware. In 1885, he replaced the wood frame building with brick. The Couse Opera House was built upstairs and completed in 1886. It is now Ward's Store, as seen in the top picture on the right.

Kingsbury County News March 1, 1889

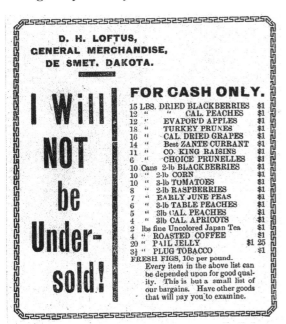

This is the southeast corner of Second Street and Calumet. The arrow points to Pa's store. Below is the same corner as it looks today.

The Ingalls and the Wilders often shopped at the Loftus Store. Today it is still located on its original site and a favorite stop for visitors to De Smet.

This picture was taken in the early 1900s and shows the northeast block of Calumet Avenue, just north of Second Street. These sheep are being taken to the stockyards. George Wilmarth owned and operated a general store at the end of the street.

On the left is the east side of Calumet Avenue during the early 1900s. The De Smet News is the first building and can still be found at its same location.

Below is the northeast corner of Calumet and Second Street. Construction began in 1888 and it is now a Bed & Breakfast.

Many advertisements were reaching De Smet about the land of Missouri. The Wilders received an apple from the Ozarks as a gift. Still looking for a better climate, they soon had "Missouri Fever" and a longing to go to the "Land of the Big Red Apple."

How did the Dakotas look in July, 1894? This newspaper article describes it well.

Yankton Press & Dakotan

July, 1894

Meteorological conditions of a phenomenal quality have existed during the present week over a wide range of western territory. Intense and protracted heat has prevailed and this oppressive period culminated yesterday in a hot south wind which sent the mercury many degrees above the hundred mark. This wind, which in some places assumed the proportions of a gale, was like a blast from a furnace and there was no haven of refuge from its debilitating effects. It was something South Dakota has never before experienced, though like of it is said to exist upon the plains of Kansas. Vegetation succumbs rapidly to such extreme heat and what was left by the long drouth had its vitality sapped by the visitation. The summer of 1894 will be long remembered in the states of the northwest for its intensity and the persistent absence of rain. Results to crop growth are disastrous. The season may be put down as an agricultural failure from the mountains to the lakes. Meteorological conditions are in sympathy with other troubles and the record of the year will be one unbroken series of disasters.

Departure day arrived. They said farewell to family and friends and headed south.

Moving Through Miner and McCook Counties

As mentioned in the introduction, it would be almost impossible to know the exact route the Wilders followed as they left De Smet. Travel routes have changed; but we decided to head south from De Smet on SD 25. We noticed that the prairie was green and not dry as mentioned in the 1894 newspaper article.

We did some exploring to the east and west of Highway 25 and talked to people in the area. We were told about the Belleview Lutheran Church that would have been seen by many pioneer travelers in the 1890s.

In the fall of 1880, Rev. E. O. Ruste, from Volga, was invited to conduct services. Because of the blizzards he was unable to arrive until June, 1881.

During the early years, there was a large horse barn on the north side. Every family had an assigned stall. Many modern improvements have been made to the church over the years and it continues to be a center of worship for area families.

BRIDGEWATER
——1880——

The Milwaukee, building from Marion to the Missouri, in 1880 soon reached Nation, platted in 1879 by Robert and J. B. Nation, with Orian K. Bullard its postmaster on 5 January 1880 and when changed to Bridgewater on November 20th he continued to serve. The election that year shifted the county seat from Cameron to Bridgewater, 119 to 109, when the canvassing board threw out 76 votes for Montrose on the pretext that it was nonexistent. The Cameron pioneers flocked to Bridgewater and to Meias, (Salem in reverse), and County Clerk H. H. Pierce took the records to the new Courthouse in Bridgewater on the corner of Poplar & 3rd Streets. Tabor & Berry, storekeepers at Cameron, shifted to Bridgewater too and had their store S of the tracks where the Shannard elevator now is located and all went through the terrific blizzard winter of 1880-81 without a train from January to April. That spring J.P. McKee's general store and W.J. Bollinger's hardware were put up on Poplar and Nation's bank at 3rd & Main. Salem won the county seat in the 1882 election. The school was moved from south of the tracks and a fine new 36 x 40 building erected in 1883 as well as the Catholic, Methodist & Presbyterian Churches. The Tribune was started in February 1881 and E.C. Kibbe ran the "Cricket" as an opposition paper. Thus for 80 years Bridgewater has been a good place to live and gets better every year.

ERECTED 1960 BY BRIDGEWATER CITY COMMISSION AND STATE HIGHWAY COMMISSION

Through Bridgewater - and on to Yankton

In 1879, this town was named Nation, in honor of Carrie Nation. One year later, the railroad workers renamed the town Bridgewater, because they had to carry their drinking water across a bridge.

Bridgewater was the home of Sparky Anderson, baseball Hall of Famer. The town now has about five hundred people and many commute to Sioux Falls for employment.

Yankton, South Dakota

Known as the "River City" Yankton was named for the tribe of Nakota (Sioux) Native Americans. They followed the river centuries ago and named the area "E-Hank-Ton-Wan.", which means "people of the end village."

Pioneer travelers going through Yankton in the 1890s saw a psychiatric hospital just west of town (built in 1882). This area, composed of several buildings, is on the National Register of Historic Places.

Burbank Building Today

Burbank Cottage, on the left, is one of the many buildings that was constructed during the 1890s. It has seen multiple uses - housing patients as well as staff offices, education, and vocational rehabilitation programs. It is now a part of the Human Services Complex.

Historic Downtown Yankton

Most of the downtown historic area was built during the late 1800s. Construction needs were met by using products from brick factories in the area. Other materials were shipped in by riverboat and train.

Today there are unique shops and restaurants, with many of the original elements still inside.

Crossing the Missouri River - at Yankton, South Dakota

From Yankton, early travelers were ferried across the river with their covered wagons and possessions.

These travelers are being ferried across the Missouri River in the late 1800s.

It became apparent that a better means of crossing the Missouri River had to be found for the town of Yankton to grow.

About 1890, a pontoon bridge was built and can be seen in the above picture.

From Yankton, South Dakota to South Yankton, Nebraska

Highway 81 crosses the Missouri River to South Yankton, Nebraska. In 1924, the Meridian Bridge was built and in 2008 the new Discovery Bridge was completed. The Meridian Bridge is now used by pedestrians and bicyclists. It is the longest pedestrian bridge in the United States.

Meridian Bridge, built in 1924
Used for 84 years

The Discovery Bridge
Completed in 2008

Hartington, Nebraska

Cedar County Courthouse

Going south, we headed toward Hartington, Nebraska, which became the county seat for Cedar County in 1885. This County Courthouse was completed in 1892 and was built with brick manufactured locally. Pioneer travelers to this area often went out of their way to get a glimpse of its Romanesque style architecture. The building is listed on the National Register of Historic Places.

The Hartington Public Library provides many services to this community as well as several surrounding communities. It has the Arlo & Anne Wirth Art Gallery with featured displays throughout the year.

During the late 1800s, Hartington became the countywide hub for retail, industrial, and professional businesses and services. Today, it continues to be the leader in these areas.

The Cedar County Historical Museum is located in a house that was donated in 1964. Another building was added and it has antique machinery, Hartington's first fire engine, and horse drawn buggies. The museum also has a log cabin and carriage house and is known as one of Cedar County's top attractions.

Stanton County and Leigh, Nebraska

Stanton County is one of the smallest out of the ninety-three in the state of Nebraska. There are only two towns, Pilger and Stanton.

Near Pilger, we saw the Elk Horn River. It is a tributary of the Platte River, one of the many rivers that travelers had to cross in the late 1800s. Seeing a shallow place in the river, we could imagine the travelers stopping for a rest and then continuing the crossing. If the river was high, they often camped until the water level subsided. This picture shows the Elk Horn River with an arrow marking a possible crossing place.

We headed west, then south, and enjoyed Stanton, the second town in this sparsely populated county. Like so many towns in Nebraska, Stanton came into being because of the Chicago & North Western Railroad. The railroad was built here in 1879 and growth began, with over twenty businesses and two new churches being established.

During the late 1800s, Stanton became a favorite stopping place for travelers since it was one of the larger towns where they could replenish their supplies for the journey. It was very progressive with the building of brick sidewalks during the 1880s and the addition of vapor gas lights in 1900.

Heritage Museum, Stanton, NE

This is the Stanton Heritage Museum which is located in the former City Hall. Built in 1918, this interesting museum was once the town fire hall and also served as a jail. There are two cells, each with two fold-down beds. The jail is in a room that provided space for the men to walk around if they were on good behavior. One can still view the prisoners' writing on the walls - names, initials, dates, etc.

Main Street, Leigh, NE

We looked at our map and the next town to the south was Leigh, just inside the Colfax County line. We found that many people in this community of about 500 are employed in Columbus and Norfolk. One of the fun highlights in this area is the Colfax County Fair, usually held during the third week of July.

Schuyler, Nebraska

Nebraska became a state in 1867. Two years later the Nebraska legislature divided Platte County into three counties and Shell Creek Station became the county seat for the new Colfax County. The next year it was renamed Schuyler.

Because of Schuyler's location along the Platte River basin, it became the crossroads for many travel routes, including the Oregon Trail, Mormon Trail, and Pony Express. The Union Pacific Railroad reached Schuyler in 1866.

Pioneers found that much of the Platte River was not navigable because of its many shallow areas. Many of them ferried across. However, many wagons crossed in the shallow areas, especially during the years of drought. Some of the shallow areas are still visible today, as seen in the picture at the right.

Today, Schuyler is a rural town of about 5000 people. Many Czech were early settlers in this area as seen by the names on buildings. German and Irish families also make up a lot of the area's population.

Cargill Meat Solutions is one of the biggest employers in the area; but many of Schuyler's populace work in Columbus, just a short distance to the west.

Lincoln, Nebraska

"Lancaster" was founded in 1864. When Nebraska became the 37th state in 1867, this town was selected as the state capital and renamed Lincoln, for former President Abraham Lincoln.

This skyscraper is the third Capitol Building in Lincoln. The first building was a two story brick structure which was made from native limestone. The building soon began to crumble.

Construction began in the early 1880s on the second Capitol Building. Again, the structure did not last and plans were made for a third Capitol Building.

The beautiful Capitol Building pictured here took over ten years to complete and was finished in 1932. The tall domed tower in the center has a 19 foot bronze figure of "The Sower."

Capitol

Building

&

"The Sower"
A

bronze

figure

at the top

of the

dome

The Governor's Mansion

Just south of the Capitol Building is a beautiful Governor's residence. The home is Georgian Colonial-style and was completed in 1957.

A mural in Haymarket Square

Historic Haymarket Square - Originally called Market Square

A favorite area in Haymarket Square

This is the section of Lincoln where wagons, hay, and camping equipment were once bought and sold. Many travelers would stop here in the 1890s for supplies.

Today it is a favorite place for people in the area as well as visitors. Unique shopping and great restaurants abound. Many buildings date back to the 1900 era.

An Early Home in Lincoln

In 1869, Secretary of State, Thomas P. Kennard, built this beautiful home. Tours are available year round and visitors learn more about life in the 1870s. Early pioneers, like the Wilders, could have passed by this house.

Kennard Home

Located At 1627 H Street

An Early Church in Lincoln

Churches have played an important role in Lincoln's history. The Wilders could have seen a church here in 1894.

First Baptist Church was founded in 1869 and has been at its same location, 1340 K Street, since 1888. At the right is a picture of the church as it looks today.

Lincoln - An Early Railroad Center

In 1870, the Burlington & Missouri River Railroad began service to the new capital city. By 1900, there were seven more railroad lines going into the city and Lincoln became a busy trading center.

Today, you will find a new Amtrak station as seen on the right. It is located near Haymarket Square.

Germans from Russia Museum

Germans from Russia Museum

Russians started coming to this area in 1874. The influence of the Germans from Russia was seen early in the history of this area. This museum shows how the early settlers lived with its German-Russian artifacts.

University of Nebraska

This university became the first in Lincoln when it was chartered in 1869. During the 1890s, there was a substantial increase in enrollment.

The first library was completed in the early 1890s and remains today as a landmark. It is now Architecture Hall.

The University Visitor Center is located at 313 N Street. They provide tours and information.

Architecture Hall is located at R Street & 10th. It is one of the many buildings constructed during the late 1800s.

The State Penitentiary in Lincoln, Nebraska

In 1870, legislation was passed to build a State Penitentiary. Within two months a temporary prison was completed and the prison opened with eighteen inmates.

The Wilders, along with many other covered wagon travelers, must have been amazed with the size and construction of this facility.

Many additions and renovations have been completed during the last 140 years and its population has averaged over 1000 in recent years.

Homestead National Monument of America

Heading south from Lincoln toward Beatrice, we were unsure of the route the Wilders followed, and decided to take US 77.

A sign marked the Homestead National Monument of America. Thinking about Laura and Almanzo's experiences with homesteading, we decided to follow US 136 west to State Highway 4.

Driving into the beautiful national monument, we found that it was located on some of the same land successfully claimed under the Homestead Act of 1862.

Homestead Act: A person could claim up to 160 acres of land if the individual resided on the land, cultivated it, and improved the property. It is estimated that some 270 million acres became privately owned under this act.

The National Park Service manages this Monument. It covers about 195 acres. The wagon in this picture is outside the Heritage Center. People enjoy this center with its pioneer exhibits, bookstore, and an interesting film.

The Palmer-Epard cabin is at the left. It was built about fourteen miles from the park and used as a home by the Palmers and Epards for over sixty years.

Freeman School is a one-room school. It was built with bricks that are one foot thick. It was used as a school from 1872-1967, the longest time for any school in this state.

Freeman School

When driving through the monument area, you will find 100 acres of tall grass prairie. There are many hiking trails of various lengths.

Beatrice, Nebraska

South on US 77 is Beatrice, the county seat for Gage County. This town has played an important role in Nebraska's history.

Many people traveled through here between 1850 and 1880 and then went on to the Oregon Trail. Flooding of the Big Blue River was a major obstacle to travel.

A dependable bridge was finally built across the Big Blue River in 1890, making travel much easier for people going through the area.

Despite its flooding the Big Blue River has provided many advantages for Beatrice, including power for the early mills and a good supply of water.

Big Blue River Bridge today

National Register of Historic Places - Gage County Courthouse

Completed in 1892, the Gage County Courthouse is listed on this National Register. Two types of stone were used in its construction - limestone and sandstone. The interior walls are made of brick, manufactured in Beatrice. It is 90 feet to the top of the tower. From there, one can see the tower of the State Capitol Building in Lincoln on a clear day. The clock at the top of the tower came from the Beatrice Post Office when it was torn down in the 1960s.

The Gage County Historical Society & Museum is housed in the 1906 Burlington Railroad Station. This station became the Gage County Historical Society in 1973 and is listed on the National Register.

Gage County Historical Society & Museum

The Union Pacific Railroad was built in the 1880s with a line between Beatrice and Marysville, Kansas. By the time the Wilders passed through here the Burlington & Missouri River Railroad had a line between Lincoln and Beatrice (constructed in 1870s). The Chicago, Rock Island & Pacific Railroad also had tracks going through Beatrice.

Chautauqua Park Tabernacle
On the National Register of Historical Places

The Chautauqua organization started in Chautauqua, NY, in 1874, and began in Beatrice about 1890. It was active in Beatrice until the 1920s. A trolley went from the town to Chautauqua Park as seen in the above picture.

Chautauqua Park Tabernacle

The Chautauqua grounds were busy as they promoted religious education, musical talents, and other interests, approaching everything with high moral standards.

Today, Chautauqua Park is still in the same location, just over the Sixth Street Bridge. The original tabernacle, still standing, is used for Homestead Days and family reunions.

Early Buildings in Beatrice

Many downtown buildings were constructed during the late 1800s and were built with stone from the Beatrice area. Pictured are a few of these buildings.

25

Marysville, Kansas

Crossing the Blue River, we arrived in Marysville. We soon found that the growth of this town, like so many, was influenced by the Big Blue River.

Marysville was a small settlement near a good crossing point on the river. In 1852, Frank Marshall moved from Missouri and operated a ferry and trading post.

To cross the river on his ferry he charged up to $5 per wagon and 25 cents per head of livestock. This settlement became known as Marshall's Ferry. In 1854, Marshall named the town Marysville, in honor of his wife.

Historic Trails Park is west of Marysville. There is a full-size replica of a rope ferry just a short distance from where Marshall had his ferry.

KANSAS HISTORICAL MARKER

MARYSVILLE

A few miles below Marysville was the famous ford on the Oregon Trail known as the Independence, Mormon or California crossing. There thousands of covered wagons with settlers bound for Oregon, Mormons for Utah and gold seekers for California crossed the Big Blue River. In 1849 a ferry and trading post was established at the ford by Frank J. Marshall, despite constant danger from Indians. Two years later the military road between Forts Leavenworth and Kearny crossed the river at the site of present Marysville, one mile west. Marshall built another ferry and for years handled an immense traffic. He gave the name of his wife, Mary, to the town that developed here and his own name to Marshall County of which it is the county seat. In 1860 Marysville became a station on the Pony Express. For most of the 1860's it was an important stopping place for coaches of the great Overland Stage Line.

Erected by Kansas Historical Society and State Highway Commission

Many trails met at this park, where they would cross the river. These trails included the Overland Stagecoach Route, Pony Express Route, Mormon Trail, and the Oregon and California Trails.

Replica of rope ferry at Historic Trails Park

National Register of Historic Places

The places shown below were built before 1894. The Wilders and other late 19th century travelers could have gone by many of them. People still enjoy touring each location and all are listed on the National Register.

Pony Express Home Station No. 1

This is the original stable for Pony Express horses. The stone barn was built in 1859. It was used during the eighteen months when the Pony Express operated, from 1860-1861. It is now a museum sharing the history of the Pony Express, early trails, and railroads around Marysville.

Charles Koester House

Charles Koester was one of the city's first bankers and built this home in 1876. It is now a museum where visitors can walk through the yard and see a dozen white bronze statues. The home is surrounded by a wall with cast iron lions and dogs guarding its gates. The inside of the home is furnished with turn-of-the-century items.

Koester House
919 Broadway

County Courthouse - Now the

Marshall County Historical Society

This Romanesque style building was completed in 1891 and replaced the previous courthouse, which had been destroyed by fire. The building has a fireproof design with its tiled floors and iron stairways. The roof is slate and galvanized iron.

This building served as the courthouse for this county for about 90 years. A new building was constructed next door and this became the Marshall County Historical Society, with a genealogical research library.

Marysville City Park

Marysville is one of the few places in Kansas where you can see black squirrels. A good place to spot these interesting animals is at the City Park, on the south edge of the town. At the park there is a 1901 Union Pacific Depot, rural schoolhouse, sod house, and a steam locomotive.

Pony Express Plaza

This plaza is located at 7th and Center. The pony express statue is over fifteen feet long and ten feet tall.

There are two murals in the plaza. The Pony Express mural is shown above. As the viewer walks, the images appear to move.

The Railroad in Marysville

The Union Pacific Railroad has had an impact on the history of this town. It employees many people and over sixty trains pass through the town every day.

A railroad underpass had to be built on US 36 because of traffic congestion.

Heading South from Marysville on US 77 - To Alcove Spring Park - on National Register of Historic Places

Trail at Alcove Spring Park

About six miles south of Marysville, on Hwy. 77, there is a sign for Alcove Spring Park. We turned on Tumbleweed Road and followed the signs.

This location was a favorite campsite along the Oregon Trail. There was a good supply of cold water and many travelers camped here while waiting for the river level to go down so they could cross.

Westmoreland, Scott Springs, & Wamego, Kansas

After visiting Alcove Spring Park, we headed toward Westmoreland, the next town on our maps. We noted the large size of the county and that Westmoreland, a town of about one thousand, is the county seat.

The county was named after the Pottawatomie Indians, a tribe that once occupied a large part of this area. This County Courthouse, built in 1884, is still being used.

Pottawatomie County Courthouse

The Rock Creek Valley Historical Society, shown on the left, is located at 507 Burkman Street. It is an excellent place to see and learn more about Pottawatomie County and Westmoreland. A railroad passenger car, buggy, and sleigh are just a few of the things shared from the 19th century.

Scott Springs, A Favorite Pioneer Camping Place

Westmoreland was a popular stopping place on the Oregon Trail. Just south of town is Scott Springs, now in Oregon Trail Park. It honors the many pioneers who camped in this area. The cold water enjoyed by the pioneers is still available here.

Old Dutch Mill Wamego, Kansas

Heading south on State Highway 99, we stopped in Wamego. People in the area said that we should see the Dutch Mill. It was built in 1879, north of town, and moved to this location in the 1920s. It grinds wheat during the Spring Tulip Festival.

Crossing the Vermillion Creek
Near Wamego, Kansas

KANSAS HISTORICAL MARKER

THE VIEUX CROSSING

A few miles to the northwest, the Oregon-California Trail crossed the Vermillion Creek, heading toward the Pacific from the "jumping off" towns on the Missouri River. The crossing was named for Louis Vieux, a Potawatomi leader of French and Native American lineage who established a toll bridge there in the 1850s. Charging a dollar per outfit, he is said to have made as much as $300 per day during busy times. In addition, he supplied emigrants with hay and grain.

As early as 1819, Thomas Say, zoologist for Stephen H. Long's expedition, camped near the crossing. John C. Fremont came in 1842, guided by Kit Carson, and in 1846 the ill-fated Donner party passed by. Beginning in 1853 the military road from Fort Leavenworth to Fort Riley crossed here, as did the stage line to Denver in 1859. Horace Greeley, a famous newspaper editor and onetime stage passenger, described a meal he had at the crossing as "the hardest I ever paid half a dollar for."

In 1849 tragedy struck when cholera took the lives of emigrants camped at the crossing. They were buried on the creekbank, as were others who died on the trail. On a nearby hill the graves of Louis Vieux, some of his family, and other early settlers can be seen in the Vieux Cemetery.

Erected by Kansas State Historical Society & Kansas Department of Transportation

Many people became entrepreneurs, building a river bridge or ferry that would handle wagons and livestock, and then offering their service to pioneer travelers. One of these enterprising individuals was Louis Vieux. He was a Pottawatomie Indian and built a bridge across the Vermillion River near Wamego. He charged one dollar per outfit and is known to have collected up to $300 per day. This historical marker is by the town of Belvue, near the place where people crossed.

St. Marys, Kansas

Our next destination was St. Marys, Kansas. We had a Kansas state map and noted that St. Marys was also on the Oregon Trail.

Travelers heading west followed that trail and would ferry across a river or wait for the river level to drop.

Many people on the trail who had gone west became discouraged. Then they headed east, toward home, using the trail.

Sometimes people on the trail were heading north or south and knew the trail would offer water and good camping.

We started wondering if the Wilders were following the Oregon Trail.

Did the Wilders Follow the Oregon Trail?

We saw the route of the Oregon Trail on the sign at the right. This was at Oregon Trail Park, south of Westmoreland. It seemed likely that the Wilders did follow a part of this trail.

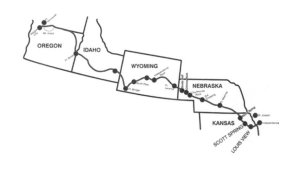

This marker showed us the importance of St. Marys on the Oregon Trail.

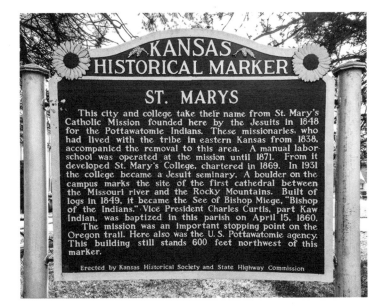

The Jesuits established a mission here in 1848, after living with the Pottawatomie Indians for ten years. They named the mission St. Mary's.

During the 1890s this town had many services to offer travelers, including a veterinarian, doctor, dentist, an elevator, lumber yard, and several general stores.

In 1857, the United States government built the Indian Pay Station to take care of business and distribute payments to the Pottawatomie Tribe. Payments were made here until 1870. This is the oldest building in Pottawatomie County and is listed on the National Register of Historic Places.

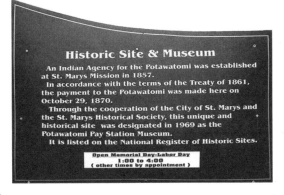

The historical barn, pictured in the background on the right, along with the Indian Pay Station, make up the St. Marys Museum Complex. The barn has many agricultural and historical items from the late 1800s. These offer a glimpse at what the Wilders could have seen on their journey through the area.

St. Mary's College - A Beautiful Landmark

In 1848, this college was founded as an Indian mission. Pioneer travelers, like the Wilders, must have enjoyed its picturesque setting and beautiful buildings. Many structures on this campus share the 1900 era.

St. Mary's College was a seminary from 1931 until 1968. In 1978, it was sold to the Society of Saint Pius X, Saint Mary's, Inc. It has no ties with the previous St. Mary's College and does not have a seminary program. It offers a K-12 and two year college curriculum.

Rossville and Silver Lake, Kansas

Rossville was founded in 1881 and named after William W. Ross. He had come to the area over thirty years before, on the Oregon Trail, and settled near St. Marys, Kansas. The town of St. Marys is about six miles to the west of Rossville and Silver Lake is to the east.

The transcontinental railway was built through this area in 1869. After that the Oregon Trail was used less than in previous years.

Rossville grew and within a couple years after its founding it had a post office, hotel, some general stores and several blacksmiths. The Kansas Valley Times newspaper was here; but moved to Topeka in 1882.

Six miles east of Rossville is Silver Lake. This town was founded in 1871, ten years before Rossville. It was also on the railroad line and Oregon Trail and became a busy town with several businesses and two large churches being built in 1878.

When the Wilders passed through this area in 1894, they could have seen many stone and sand buildings, since both were plentiful in the area.

Today the Town Library, shown here, occupies one of the buildings erected in Silver Lake during the late 1800s. Through the years the building has seen many uses, including a grocery store and several other retail businesses.

A Few Facts About the Oregon Trail

The trail spanned 2000 miles and crossed six states - Missouri, Kansas, Nebraska, Wyoming, Idaho, and Oregon. Because of its many offshoots, it became known by many names, including California Trail, Mormon Trail, and Platte Trail. The trail was also used by the Army and Pony Express. It is estimated that over 400,000 settlers used the trail.

Topeka, Kansas

As early as 1842, Topeka was a busy town. Joseph and Louis Papin operated Papin's Ferry that crossed the Kansas River. In 1849-1850, many people were headed to California and crossed on this ferry. The trail took on another name, the California Trail, since so many people were headed in that direction.

In 1857, a bridge was built across the Kansas River. The bridge, pictured below, was used by many travelers in 1894. This photo was taken about 1870.

The sign above the bridge reads, "No person allowed to ride or drive over the bridge faster than a walk or have on more than 50 head of cattle at one time."

The number of cattle allowed was later changed to 25. The iron structure was replaced in 1898 by the Melan Bridge.

Photo at the right shows the present Kansas Avenue Bridge. Construction on this bridge began in 1964, before the Melan Bridge collapsed in 1965. This new bridge was finished in 1967.

By the late 1800s the train had become a popular means of travel throughout the Midwest.

This Railway Time Table was in an Ottawa newspaper on August 20, 1894.

Today, the Amtrak Station, pictured below, provides service to many areas.

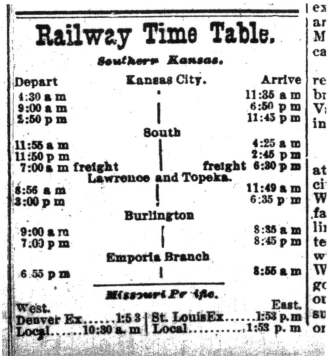

Kansas Museum of History in Topeka

The Kansas Museum of History offers a great opportunity to learn more about the past years of this interesting state.

The museum has seven sections.

Early People	5,000 B.C. - 1820 A.D.
Trails	1820 -1860
Civil War	1861 -1865
Settling the Frontier	1865 -1880
Trains & Towns	1880 -1900
Early 20th Century	1900 -1940
Recent Past	1940 -1990

There is a hands-on gallery called Discovery Place and a 2.5 mile nature trail.

Capitol Building in Topeka

The picture on the left was taken in 1893, during construction of the dome. The Capitol work began in 1866 and was finally completed in 1903. The Wilders and other 1894 travelers could have passed here during construction.

On the right is a picture of the present Capitol Building dome in Topeka.

In 2002 the bronze sculpture shown on the left was added at the top of the dome. This sculpture shows a Kansas Native American with bow and arrow pointed at the North Star. The bronze sculpture weighs over four thousand pounds.

Topeka - A Place With So Much to See From the Past

Topeka has many buildings still standing from the 1890s and offers great opportunities for learning more about the era when the Wilders journeyed through this area.

Old Prairie Town at Ward-Meade Historic Site

This pioneer village is located along what used to be the Oregon Trail. All the buildings originated before 1900. A mansion, built in the 1870s, is on the National Register of Historic Places.

General Store

This six-acre historic site provides beautiful photo backgrounds for families, weddings, clubs, and special occasions.

Everyone enjoys the livery stable, Santa Fe Depot and Caboose, 1891 one-room school, museum, Mulvane General Store, and gift shop.

An Early Fire Station in Topeka

Fire Station No. 4 is located at 813 Clay Street and is still being used today.

Fire Station No. 4 - Today

Fire Station No. 4 - Photo from 1890s

37

Historic Homes in Topeka

The red brick home on the left is the John Ritchie House, built in 1856. It was made from materials he had left over after constructing a commercial block in Topeka. It is considered Topeka's oldest home and was a station along the Underground Railroad. His son, Hale, became owner of the house in 1875.

In 1886, Hale built the house shown to the right of the first house. Today this home is being reconditioned into a service center to support heritage programs of the Shawnee County Historical Society.

Charles Curtis was the 31st Vice President of the United States and built this home in 1879. He was the only U. S. Vice President of Native American heritage. It is considered one of the great historic landmarks of Topeka and is on the National Register of Historic Places.

Travelers in the 1890s, like the Wilders, could have passed all three of these homes.

First Presbyterian Church

This church was organized in 1859. The present building is their third and was built in 1884. People from all over the world have come to view their Tiffany windows, installed in 1911.

Towns of the Past

In 1894, when the Wilders passed through Richland, it was a busy town with about three hundred people. The town was established in the 1850s and a post office and log schoolhouse constructed in 1857.

Wagon travelers passing through this town in the 1890s were happy to find two blacksmiths and two doctors. A general store gave them a chance to replenish supplies. The town even had a newspaper.

Like so many towns, the railroad was an asset to Richland's growth since it was a stop on the St. Louis to Denver route. However, the railroad stopped running in 1894 and the town declined.

The Army Corps of Engineers acquired the land in this area for flood control. During the late 1960s and early 1970s, the town was abandoned. The post office closed in 1969 and today little remains of Richland, except pieces of broken pavement that were once the town's streets.

More Towns Disappear

There had been many floods in the valley of the Wakarusa River. It became necessary to build a dam, creating Clinton Lake. Richland was one of the many towns that disappeared. Others included Sigil, Belvoir, and Bloomington.

The Wakarusa River flows through the Clinton Dam south of Lawrence and on to the Kansas River with several tributaries. It is difficult to see towns disappear; but the Clinton Dam has had many positive effects. It is a source of water for thousands of people in northeastern Kansas.

Clinton Lake has turned into a busy recreation area and the parks are managed by the Army Corps of Engineers. Boating, fishing, camping and picnicking, along with hiking and biking trails, make it a popular place for all ages.

The mural at the right depicts the history of this area. It is at the Clinton Lake Visitor Center.

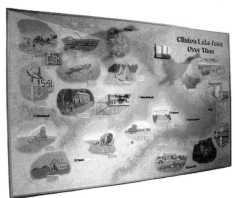

Clinton Lake Corps of Engineers Visitor Center
Artist Randall Bennett

Kansas - Summer of 1894

The summer of 1894 was very dry throughout the Midwest. Newspaper articles depicted what it was like. This appeared in the Ottawa Daily Tribune during the third week of August in 1894. The welcome rains were starting to come.

Farmers are in a constant condition of worry over hedges. The dry weather has been productive of an unusual quantity of the flying debris of the plains known as "tumble weed," which collects along the hedge rows, and being dry as tinder is easily fired. Scores of fine hedges have been ruined by fire in this way.

The rain of Tuesday morning was general over the county, and in places heavy. In the north-west corner about three-fourths of an inch fell. The western and south-western townships were even better favored, and in Richmond the fall was fully one and a half inches. Four miles north of the city the fall was heavier than it was in town.

Miss Wright has been having fun with

Ottawa, Kansas

Historic District-Downtown Ottawa

The structures on Ottawa's Main Street were built between 1872 and 1900. The Wilders, and others traveling through the area in 1894, could have replenished some of their supplies at the stores located here. Much of the area is listed on the National Register of Historic Places.

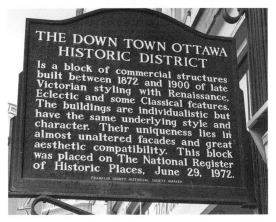

Kiosks - A Great Historical Sharing in Ottawa

Ottawa has eight kiosks and we thought they were one of the best ways for a town to share its history. Many of these kiosks are on Main Street.

You can look at an old photo of a building and then look to see what is there today. The photos have interesting background information. Two of these kiosks can be seen on page 44.

Early Travelers and Buyers in Ottawa, Kansas

During the 1890s travelers, like the Wilders, found Ottawa a great place to replenish their supplies. Here is an advertisement from one of the stores on Main Street.

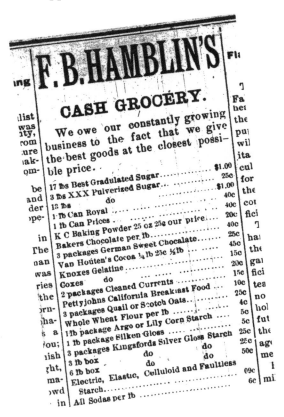

Some buildings along today's Main Street

This advertisement, appearing in the Ottawa Daily Republican on August 20, 1894, shows some of the items that were available and their prices.

Marais des Cygnes River

This river is about 140 miles long and flows through the counties of Osage, Franklin, Miami, and Linn. There were major floods in these areas and the water crested over 36 feet (1902); 31 feet (1915); 38 feet (1928); and 42 feet (1951).

During the 1960s the U S Army Corps of Engineers built levees and flood control systems. The present levee is seen at the right.

Franklin County Courthouse - Ottawa, Kansas

Franklin County Courthouse - Completed in 1893
Listed on National Register of Historic Places

Travelers going through this area in 1894 must have been very impressed by the stature of this building. The courthouse measures 73 feet by 112 feet, with a full basement, three floors, and an intricate roof design. The cornerstone ceremonies were held on July 4, 1892, and the building was dedicated on Oct. 3,1893. It took less than two years to complete, a marvel, even by today's standards.

All building supplies for the courthouse were found nearby. Limestone for the walls was shipped from the Rettiger Quarry, Strong City; red-faced brick was made by Ottawa Brick & Tile; sandstone was shipped from Warrensburg, Missouri.

Total cost of building $49,014.69
Heating, plumbing,
light fixtures, furniture $17, 924,56
          Total $66,939.25

The building still has its original staircase and trim. It is one of the thirteen Kansas courthouses, along with several Carnegie Libraries, designed by George P. Washburn. Eleven of these courthouses are still standing today and many of them are listed on the National Register of Historic Places.

One of the tower displays has a four-sided clock and another one has a large bell.

Across from the County Courthouse are the buildings on the left. These were constructed between 1887 and 1892. People visiting this area in 1894 would marvel at the courthouse and would also be surprised by the new commercial buildings across the street.

Old Depot Museum

&

Another

Interesting

Kiosk

This railroad depot is made of limestone and was built in 1888. It was a busy place in 1894. It is another Ottawa building that was designed by George P. Washburn and is listed on the National Register.

The building was given to the Franklin County Historical Society in 1962. Today it offers a look at early life in Kansas and includes a general store, one-room school, and a model railroad.

The railroad line no longer serves Ottawa. The track has been made into the Prairie-Spirit Rail-Trail, a 51 mile trail from Ottawa to Iola that is enjoyed by hikers and bikers.

Dietrich Cabin

In

The

Ottawa

City Park

The Dietrichs had moved west from Chicago and built this cabin in 1859. It was located southwest of Princeton in Franklin County.

The cabin is about 18 feet by 20 feet and is made from native walnut. The cabin was near the Humboldt Trail and the 8 foot porch became a resting place for travelers who stopped by for food and shelter. Eventually the cabin was abandoned and the dwelling used to store hay.

In 1959, a granddaughter gave the cabin to the Franklin County Historical Society. It was moved to Ottawa City Park and restored in 1960-61. It stands as a tribute to early pioneers and is also listed on the National Register of Historic Places.

Lane, Kansas

People passing through Lane in 1894, like the Wilders, would enjoy a large hardware for replenishing their supplies. The town also had a hotel and blacksmith with a livery stable.

Just north of Lane is the Pottawatomie Creek. In 1856, a band of abolitionists, led by John Brown, murdered five pro-slavery men. This massacre in "Bleeding Kansas" was one of the most famous events leading up to the Civil War.

John Brown was later captured, tried, and hanged, in 1859, for his unsuccessful raid on Harper's Ferry, in West Virginia.

With an abundance of limestone in the area, many homes were built from this material in the late 1800s. One can still see several of these places around Lane.

Today, many people from this area work in Paola. Some even drive as far as Kansas City for employment.

Part of Main Street
Lane, Kansas - 2013

Limestone home, Lane area

Mound City, Kansas

This town became the county seat in 1875 and the courthouse was finished near the end of 1886. It is the second oldest courthouse still in use in Kansas and also on the National Register of Historic Places.

Most of the materials needed for its construction came from the Linn County area. These included red brick, limestone, and flagstone.

Six offices on the main floor were heated with individual coal stoves until 1931.

Mound City Historical Park

This Historical Park is sponsored by the Mound City Historical Society. Located on Highway 52 West, all the structures have been moved or reconstructed here. Among the buildings you will find a one-room school that was used from 1868-1959.

Mound City once had the Missouri Pacific Railroad. The depot is now part of this park with many old-time displays. One of the favorite places in the park is the Clawson log cabin. It dates back to the late 1800s and was used for 45 years.

This block of Main Street was built during the 1800s. The Opera House was a favorite place in the 1890s.

Woodland Cemetery has a National Cemetery Plot. In 1864, this started with 30 union soldiers, killed in two different battles.

 Mound City Hall was built in 1868 and still stands on Main Street.

In 1889, the United States erected the Union Soldiers monument to honor the 80 Civil War soldiers laid to rest at the Mound City Soldiers' Lot.

The Sugar Mound Arts & Crafts Festival is held in October at the Linn County Fairgrounds. Craft and food booths and an Antique Barn are featured.

Prescott, Kansas

This town was originally called Coal Centre; but the railroad changed the name to Prescott, since they already had a Coal Centre.

The school was built in 1883 and used until 1972. Like so many schools in rural Kansas, it was the center of community activities. Today it is the Prescott Library. The building is on the National Register of Historic Buildings.

In July, this area celebrates Coal Center Days, featuring a parade and fun activities.

Fort Scott, Kansas

A walk or drive through Fort Scott's Historic District makes one realize what a busy place this must have been in 1894. Travelers enjoyed the many stores for purchasing their needs.

Checking the dates on buildings, and noting the architecture, it is apparent that many were built during the late 1800s. During this time Fort Scott was competing with Kansas City as one of the busiest railroad centers west of the Mississippi. At one time there was even talk about Fort Scott becoming the state's capital.

Today, this historic district continues to be a center for many business activities.

Old Market Square has a Farmer's Market on Tuesdays and Saturdays. In this area, a trolley tour of the town is offered during several months.

Fort Scott National Historic Site

This is the Fort Scott Visitor Center and Bookstore. During the 1840s it was the hospital, where surgeons treated the sick and wounded soldiers. An upstairs hospital ward has been refurnished.

Dragoon Stables
Eighty horses with their feed, tack, and hay could be sheltered here.

Dragoon Barracks
Soldiers slept on the second floor and ate on the first floor.

Officers' Quarters

Between 1842 and 1846 a lot of this fort was built by the soldiers themselves - barracks, stables, a hospital, and several storehouses. The purpose for the fort was to maintain peace between the Native American tribes, local tribes, and incoming settlers. Money ran out and work on the fort ended in 1850.

Kansas became a state in 1861. Even though entering as a "free state" there was a tremendous pro-slavery movement. This controversy and the battles that followed gave it the nickname, "bleeding Kansas."

The U S Army returned to Fort Scott in 1861 and this fort became its headquarters. Records show that at one time the post had 400 horses and 460 men. This had a great impact on the town which had many well-stocked stores and even a hotel.

Today, the Fort Scott National Historic Site is maintained by the National Park Service. There are guided and self-guided tours as well as a Visitor Center & Bookstore. Over a dozen buildings can be photographed with many different types of architecture.

Fort Scott National Cemetery

During the early days of Fort Scott the Army established a cemetery on the west side of the town. In 1861, approximately four acres were purchased, southeast of the Fort Scott Post, for use as a community burying ground. It was controlled by the Presbyterian Church and became known as the Presbyterian Graveyard.

In 1862 the Presbyterian Graveyard and an adjoining tract, owned by the Town Company, were designated as Fort Scott National Cemetery. It now covers 21.8 acres. This is one of our country's fourteen original national cemeteries and is on the National Register of Historic Places.

The Gordon Parks Museum Center for Culture and Diversity

Gordon Parks was the youngest of fifteen children and left Fort Scott when he was sixteen, after his mother died. He went on to become the first African-American photographer for Life Magazine.

He authored many books, including *Learning Tree*, where he wrote about his hometown. He wrote musical compositions and directed several films, including *The Learning Tree* and *Shaft*.

Gordon Parks had to overcome many barriers; but he was able to achieve success, both artistically and professionally. He has often been called "The Renaissance Man."

This museum, located at Fort Scott Community College, shares several of his magazine articles, musical compositions, and photographs that exhibit his creative genius.

Personal items, including his writing desk and posters, can be seen. Many of his books and other souvenirs are available at the museum store.

Lamar, Missouri

Birthplace of Harry S. Truman, Our 33rd President

The house has been furnished with décor from the 1800s, like the butter churn and pedal sewing machine at the right.

The Truman family had moved into this house in November, 1882. On May 8, 1884, Harry S. Truman was born here. The Trumans remained in Lamar until March of 1885. Then the family moved to Harrisonville, Missouri.

When the Trumans lived here, the house had no electricity, running water, or bathroom. When you visit the property today, you can still see the deep cistern.

In 1957, the United Auto Workers purchased this property and gave it to the people of Missouri. It is operated and maintained by the Division of Parks and Recreation for the State of Missouri.

Square & Courthouse - Lamar, Missouri

The Square is in the center of Lamar with the first buildings being constructed in the 1860s. The Trumans probably spent some time here since many more buildings were erected before their departure in 1885.

By 1890 half of the buildings in the Square were completed. The Wilders could have seen a lot of activity as they passed through the area. Like other 1894 travelers, they would see this beautiful Barton County Courthouse, built in 1888, in the center of the Square. The Courthouse is still used today.

Barton County Courthouse
Historic Picture from 1900 era

Barton County Courthouse today

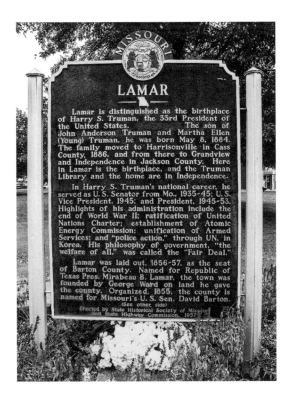

Located on the courthouse lawn, this plaque marks the place where Truman delivered his vice-presidential acceptance speech on August 31, 1944.

The Barton County Courthouse lawn has many interesting items from history. These include the historical sign and Truman Memorial.

The Square - Lamar, Missouri
Comparing the Past & the Present

West Side of Square, 1905

West Side of Square, Today

The store on the southern most end of the block is the jewelry store of John Earp, first cousin to Wyatt Earp. John Earp is standing alone in front of his store. He has his arms to his side.

Next to the jewelry store is the Diamond Drug Company. Above the drug company is C. R. Taylor's Photo Gallery. Its convenient stopping point, along with a variety of stores, made this area a popular place for travelers in the late 1800s.

North Side of Square, 1905

North Side of Square, Today

Both of the historic photos on this page were taken by C. R. Taylor. He had the photographer's gallery above the Diamond Drug Store from 1898 until 1912.

This area continues to be a busy business center, with specialty shops, services, and restaurants.

Golden City, Missouri

We headed east from Lamar on Highway 160 through an area called "Golden Grove."

Apparently this name stems from gold mining stories, some probably true and others untrue. Many of these tales go back for hundreds of years.

During the 1860s this town started growing when a general store, post office, and blacksmith shop were constructed. During the next decade a hotel, drugstore, and several other businesses were added.

Main Street Today in Golden City, Missouri

Like so many places in Missouri, the railroad line had an impact on this town. Golden City became a stop in 1880 with the building of the Kansas City/Fort Scott & Gulf Railroad. By 1881 the town was booming as many more businesses flourished. Now, building materials could come by rail instead of being hauled by wagon from neighboring towns.

More grocery stores were built and more doctors moved into the area. A shoe store and photograph shop were started. The town also had a newspaper.

During the late 1800s a Baptist Church was organized. They are still meeting at the same location on Highway 160. The bell on the front lawn is from the original church.

Another
View
of
Main Street
Golden City,
Missouri

If the Wilders had stopped here to purchase land, they would have seen these prices in 1894: 8 acres/$600; 14 acres/$700; 80 acres/$2000.

Lockwood and Greenfield, Missouri

Main Street today in Lockwood

Like so many towns in western Missouri, Lockwood's growth was influenced by the railroad. The town was named after J. E. Lockwood, who was the general-passenger agent for the railroad. People working on the railroad gave this town the nickname, "The Queen City of the Prairie."

Because of the railroad several hotels were built. These were needed for the many traveling salesmen and workers coming to the town.

When the Wilders passed through here in 1894, they would have seen a flourishing town with farm produce being sent out by rail. Many businesses offered provisions for travelers. The first telephone line was planned and service began in 1895.

Greenfield - County Seat for Dade County

In the mid 1800s, Greenfield became a town and plans were made for the courthouse and town square.

Visitors to this area in the late 1800s would have enjoyed a busy town. There were many businesses and even an Opera House. This building is still being used for some summer productions.

Because of its abundance of water in streams and springs, the area was very attractive to people from states east of here looking for a place to settle.

Opera House   Built in 1888

Main Street, Greenfield, MO

Three churches were built during the late 1800s and early 1900s. Some original buildings are still being used today. The church at the right was established in 1839.

Cumberland Presbyterian Church

Dade County Today

The Wilders would have seen the third courthouse, built in 1868. The present building was constructed in 1928, and has this memorial to veterans.

Hulston Mill

While in Greenfield, we asked some people, "What was in this area in 1894?" Their consistent reply, "Hulston Mill." Getting directions from them, we headed east on Highway 160, north on State Rd. EE, and then east on County Road 92.

We were told that Hulston Mill was originally built about a mile northwest of here in 1840. However, with the construction of Stockton Lake, the mill had to be moved.

In 1894, the Hulston family still owned this mill. The Wilders would have seen a busy place with an auxiliary steam engine providing power when there was a drought.

Hulston Mill

Today it is a 50-acre park, managed by the Dade County Historical Society and enjoyed by all ages. Camping is available and children like the antique playground equipment. There are three log cabins and an amphitheatre. The equestrian trails are popular and the Hulston Mill still operates.

An early log cabin at the park

1894 - Springfield, Missouri

Springfield was a booming business center by the 1890s and construction was very eminent. This beautiful building was being built in 1894, as the Wilders passed through the area. It was built to serve as a U. S. Customhouse and Post Office at a cost of $133,000.

Today, it houses The History Museum for Springfield-Greene County, with displays telling the history of this area. Their quilts, costumes, china, furniture, and household items show the many changes over the past century.

Town Square - The Historic Center of Springfield

The town square has been the center of business activity and historic events from the very beginning of the city. It was the location for some early stage routes. These pictures were taken around 1900.

The town square made national news in 1865. The story is told that David Tutt and Bill Hickok had a disagreement over a poker game and Tutt took Hickok's pocket watch.

The next day they met in the Square. Tutt fired at Hickok and missed him. Hickok fired back and killed Tutt. This event was highly publicized. "Wild Bill Hickok" was arrested and later freed.

The above pictures show some of Park Central Square as it looks today. The area was recently renovated and has several specialty shops and restaurants. It provides unique backgrounds for pictures and is a great place to relax.

Springfield in the Late 1800s
A Busy Railroad Center

In 1870, the St. Louis-San Francisco Railroad Line rolled through the area and a town, "North Springfield," emerged. North Springfield and Springfield joined in 1887 to become the one town of Springfield. Soon there were over 150 businesses operating and it became known as "Queen City of the Ozarks."

When the Wilders passed through here in 1894, they would have seen a busy business center as well as a town with woolen, cotton, and flour mills. The convenience of railroad shipping had added to this thrust in business.

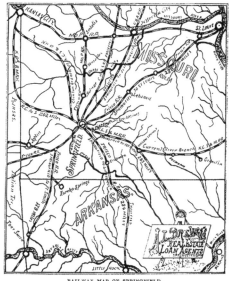

SPRINGFIELD, MISSOURI, AND SURROUNDINGS • 1889

RAILWAY MAP OF SPRINGFIELD.

Today, we can get a good view of the railroad tracks, which are still in use, from the Jefferson Avenue Footbridge. This is also on the National Register of Historic Places.

Railroad Historical Museum

Located in Grant Beach Park, this unique museum is actually inside a Frisco 4524 locomotive, a Burlington Baggage Car, a Chicago Northwestern Commuter Car, and the Burlington Northern Caboose. There are many hands-on activities for children.

There are many photos, paintings, and equipment displays showing the history of the railroad and its importance to Springfield.

57

Places Viewed By Travelers in 1894

The Wilders could have seen any of these places since all were in the same location as they are today and very visible in 1894. All are listed on the National Register of Historic Places.

Springfield National Cemetery

In 1867, the Springfield National Cemetery was erected. Soldiers from the North and South were interred here. At that time they were separated by a low stone wall.

Heroes from all wars are buried here. These include hundreds of Civil War soldiers killed during the Battle of Pea Ridge, Battle of Wilson's Creek, and the Battle of Springfield. Several special monuments have been erected in memory of fallen heroes. The first one was erected in 1888 in memory of General Nathaniel Lyon, who was killed at the Battle of Wilson's Creek.

Stone Chapel - Drury University

Construction of the Stone Chapel started in 1880; but it was gutted by a fire in 1882, before completion. It was rebuilt and completed in 1892 and is the oldest stone structure in Springfield. The chapel is located on the Drury University campus and is used for many of the university's activities.

Christ Episcopal Church

Christ Episcopal
Church
is located at
601 East Walnut

This is the oldest church in Springfield. It was founded in 1859 with the building being completed in 1870. Additions have been made to the church; but the original building was saved. Its architecture is a beautiful example of adding the new; but still keeping the old.

Walnut Street Historic District

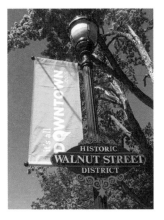

Thirteen blocks make up this historic area and many of the homes were here before 1900. The Queen Anne style of architecture is prominent in several places.

The first homes in this area, prior to 1900, were built by people involved in the early growth of Springfield - bankers, manufacturers, and merchants. Many elements in the buildings are from the late 1800s: brick and stone walks; carriage blocks; shakes and shingles; along with windows of leaded and stained glass.

The two homes pictured here were built in 1892 and 1893. People traveling during the 1890s would often pass these places, both located on Walnut Street.

The home on the right was built by George Anderson, an Ozarks lumber baron. The one on the left was built by Edward Mosher. He was owner of the United Iron Works.

Early Trolleys & Transportation in Springfield

The Town Square, now called Park Central Square, has been a center for Springfield's transportation from the town's early beginning. In 1858, the Butterfield Overland Stage Coach stopped at a station on the northeast corner.

As early as 1887, Springfield became one of the first cities to get an electric trolley. By the 1890s there were lines going to different parts of the town. This was a convenience and also provided fun for all ages. The streetcars continued to be used until 1937 when they were replaced by busses. The depression also had its influence on their decline.

SPRINGFIELD, MISSOURI, AND SURROUNDINGS • 1889

H. M. HECKART'S JEWELRY STORE, PUBLIC SQUARE.

Mansfield, Missouri

In 1881, F. M. Mansfield and George H. Nettleton purchased the town site. Mansfield was an attorney in Hartville, about twelve miles to the north. Nettleton was a railroad surveyor from Kansas City.

1882 - A Year of Growth

The railroad was built through Mansfield in 1882 and the town business activity greatly increased. A post office was established along with several general stores.

Mansfield became the "Crossroads of the Ozarks" as its location made it a distribution center from Grovespring, approximately 25 miles north, to the Arkansas state line, about 50 miles south.

The village of Mansfield was officially incorporated in 1886. By that time, Mansfield already had its first church and school and the city council authorized the building of wooden sidewalks.

In the late 1800s, F. M. Mansfield, built this home, which is still standing today.

Busy Mansfield & the Railroad

The railroad made Mansfield a busy shipping point and many companies emerged during the late 1880s and through the 1890s. Records show that zinc and lead were mined and shipped from the area.

The Mansfield Bank was established in 1892 on Commercial Street. The picture at the left was taken during the late 1890s. The Wilders were frequent patrons.

Mansfield Bank
Late 19th Century

Bank of Mansfield Today - Still at its original location on Commercial Street

A Church & School in Early Mansfield

The Wilders had always attended a Congregational Church. Laura was disappointed to find that Mansfield did not have a Congregational Church. The Wilders attended the Methodist Church pictured on the right.

This was Mansfield's first school, which was organized in the 1880s. It is now a private residence.

Mansfield Methodist Church
About 1900

A Busy Town Square in Mansfield

The Town Square has always been a busy place. There is no doubt that the Wilders probably heard about many of the festivals and events being held there and might have enjoyed attending some of them.

This photo was taken about 1900.

It shows ladies dressed up for the Mansfield Carnival & Stock Show. The busy stores are visible in the background, as well as the wooden sidewalks and unpaved streets.

Mansfield Town Square - Then & Now

This photo was taken in the early 1900s showing the east side of the Mansfield Town Square. The Bank of Mansfield is seen on the left, at the north end of the Square. Musicians are entertaining and one can still see the unpaved streets.

East Side of the Town Square as it looks today

This photo shows a holiday parade in Mansfield in the early 1900s.

Wilder Days Festival in Mansfield - An Annual September Event

The Town Square features many craft booths, contests, games and entertainment. A parade highlights the weekend as people come from several neighboring states to enjoy the festivities. There is something special for all ages.

Those attending Laura Days also enjoy "Laura's Memories," presented by the Ozark Mountain Players. It is an outdoor musical pageant based on the life of Laura Ingalls Wilder, and shares excerpts from her many books.

Mansfield - An Interesting Place to Visit Today

Mansfield Historical Society
is located at
111 West Park Square.

Carl Mays is honored in the
Town Square. He was a
professional ballplayer.

Laura sold her eggs
at the Farmers Exchange.
This building is
still located on Hwy. A

Honoring Laura
In the Town Square

Mansfield
Historical Society
has many
interesting displays.

On the right is
their display of
blacksmith tools.

Near Town
Square is the
Seal home.
The Seals
were close
friends of the
W i l d e r s .
They often
t r a v e l e d
together.

Seal Home

Laura Ingalls Wilder Library
A short distance from the
Town Square

Almanzo is sitting in the buggy, obtained by the Wilders after reaching Mansfield. The horses are the team that pulled them from De Smet, South Dakota to Mansfield, Missouri.

The log house in the background is where they lived during their first winter in Mansfield. The Wilders had purchased this house and 40 acres shortly after their arrival in Mansfield in 1894.

Rose, with her donkey, Spookendyke. She rode him to school and described him as the "stubborn donkey."

Almanzo is working the land during one of their early years at Rocky Ridge Farm.

Laura and Almanzo, with Jim Wilson and a hired hand, on the porch at Rocky Ridge Farm.

This picture was in the Missouri Ruralist, June 1, 1912. Almanzo is standing by one of his 12 year old apple trees. The Wilders had been in Mansfield about 18 years. They had started with 40 and now had 100 acres. By 1912, this was all paid for and doubled in value. He was known to have one of the best apple orchards in this part of Missouri.

Rocky Ridge Farm Today

In 1894, Laura and Almanzo purchased 40 acres of land and Laura named it "Rocky Ridge Farm." Eventually the farm grew to about 200 acres. They added on to their original home with the last addition being completed in 1913. The house was built with materials from the land.

Laura started writing her Little House books while living in Rock House. (page 70) After living in Rock House for eight years, Laura and Almanzo returned to their Rocky Ridge Home. Laura continued writing and finished *By the Shores of Silver Lake* (1939). *The Long Winter* (1940); *Little Town on the Prairie* (1941); and *These Happy Golden Years* (1943).

Most of the rooms at Rocky Ridge Farm have been kept almost as they were at the time of Laura's death. As you enter the home, there is a screened-in porch, a comfortable place to eat during the hot summers. A door leads into the kitchen.

The cupboards and work area are low in the kitchen. These were built by Almanzo for Laura's short stature.

Laura, Almanzo, and their dog, Nero, are in front of Rock House. This home was a Christmas gift from their daughter, Rose, in 1928. This is where Laura started writing the Little House Books.

Rock House

Rose Wilder lived with Almanzo's sister, Eliza Jane, and attended high school in Crowley, Louisiana. She graduated in 1904.

In 1908, she started working for the San Francisco Bulletin and her reputation as a writer became widespread. During the 1920s she returned to Mansfield. In 1928, Rose gave her parents the keys to Rock House, a beautiful home just down the hill from Rocky Ridge.

While living in Rock House, Laura started writing the Little House Books. Her first book, *Little House in the Big Woods,* was published in 1932. She then wrote three more books: *Farmer Boy* (1933), *Little House on the Prairie* (1935), and *On the Banks of Plum Creek* (1937).

After living here for eight years, Laura and Almanzo moved back to Rocky Ridge Farm and Laura continued her writing.

This is how Rock House looks today. Visitors from all over the world enjoy tours of the home. The garage, pictured below, is behind Rock House. This is where Almanzo and Laura parked their Chrysler.

Find out more about all of these places on pages 72 - 77.

1. LIW Memorial Society
  Pepin, WI 54759
www.lauraingallspepin.com

2. LIW Memorial Society, Inc.
  De Smet, SD 57231
www.discoverlaura.org
2. Ingalls Homestead
  De Smet, SD 57231
www.ingallshomestead.com

3. Laura Ingalls Wilder Museum
  Walnut Grove, MN 56180
www.walnutgrove.org

4. Little House on the Prairie Museum
  Independence, KS 67301
www.littlehouseontheprairiemuseum.com

5. Wilder Home Assoc. Malone, NY 12953
www.almanzowilderfarm.com

Plan to Visit these Little House Places

NORTH DAKOTA
MINNESOTA
SOUTH DAKOTA
WISCONSIN
2 3 8 1
11
6
IOWA
10 9
NEBRASKA
MISSOURI
KANSAS
4 7

1. Pepin, WI   7. Mansfield, MO
2. De Smet, SD   8. Spring Valley, MN
3. Walnut Grove, MN   9. West Branch, IA
4. Independence, KS   10. Vinton, IA
5. Malone, NY   11. Keystone, SD
6. Burr Oak, IA

6. LIW Park & Museum
  Burr Oak, IA 52101
www.lauraingallswilder.us

7. LIW & RWL Museum & Home
  Mansfield, MO 65704
www.lauraingallswilderhome.com

8. Spring Valley Community Historical Soc.
  Spring Valley, MN 55975
springvalleymnmuseum.com

9. Herbert Hoover Library
  West Branch, IA 52358
http://hoover.archives.gov

10. Iowa Braille School
  Vinton, IA 52349
www.iowa-braille.k12.ia.us

11. Keystone Area Historical Society
  Keystone, SD 57751
www.keystonehistory.com

Visit our website www.lhsitetours.homestead.com
Email: lhsitetours@email.com

Pepin, Wisconsin

In her book, *Little House in the Big Woods*, Laura describes her childhood years in Pepin, Wisconsin. Today, people enjoy visiting "Little House Wayside." A replica cabin was built in 1976 and replaced by the cabin (pictured on left) in 1992.

Two museums are located on Main Street. The Depot Museum, (center picture) has displays about early railroading, as well as logging and boating on Lake Pepin. Pepin Historical Museum, on the right, features rooms with items from local history and exhibits about Laura Ingalls Wilder. It is managed by the LIW Memorial Society.

Burr Oak, Iowa

Masters Hotel

Laura never mentions Burr Oak in her books. It comes between her stories, *On the Banks of Plum Creek* and *By the Shores of Silver Lake*.

Burr Oak Bank Building

The Ingalls family moved here, during the fall of 1876, to help the Steadmans run the Masters Hotel. Laura and Mary helped Ma with the daily chores at the hotel. Grace, the youngest of the Ingalls' daughters, was born here on May 23, 1877.

The Masters Hotel has been restored and offers an interesting tour of its eleven rooms. A visitor sees many 19th century household items and a pipe organ from the 1880s.

Across from the Masters Hotel is the Burr Oak Bank Building. This was built in 1910 and served the Burr Oak community until 1932.

The Bank Building is now a Visitor Center and Gift Shop for the Laura Ingalls Wilder Park and Museum.

De Smet, South Dakota - Setting for Five Little House Books

In this book, pages 6 through 12, you will find a brief history of this interesting town. There is a picture of the Ingalls Home (page 8). Stop by the Gift Shop on Olivet Avenue, shown in the picture on the right. Here you can learn more about touring the Ingalls Home, Brewster School, De Smet's first school, and the Surveyor's House, where the Ingalls' family spent their first winter in De Smet.

The Ingalls Homestead, located southeast of De Smet, is a fun place with many pioneer activities.

Little House activities are experienced at Flindts Garage. These include the twisting of hay, grinding of wheat seed, and making corncob dolls.

For three weekends in July, De Smet has a pageant, with Pa's cottonwoods in the background and a setting sun in the west. This scenery shows an evening pageant and the sharing of a Little House Book.

Pump water and have a cold drink.

Ride a covered wagon to the one-room school.

Walnut Grove, Minnesota

The Ingalls family left Pepin, Wisconsin, in 1874 and moved to Walnut Grove, Minnesota. The only housing Pa could find for his family was a dugout site on Plum Creek.

Today, this dugout site is a favorite stop for visitors to the area. People enjoy wading in Plum Creek, just like Laura!

Walnut Grove has a "hands-on" museum, a favorite place for photos. There are many items from Laura's era along with pictures and memorabilia from the TV series.

Pa gave his last three dollars so the church could have a bell, now seen at the English Lutheran Church.

Fragments of a Dream
Pageant Scenery

For three weekends in July, local volunteers present an outdoor pageant, *Fragments of a Dream.* This story shares Laura's life in Walnut Grove.

Spring Valley, Minnesota

Spring Valley Church Museum

Many people wonder why Almanzo's parents, James and Angeline Wilder, moved to Spring Valley. They had visited the farm, owned by Angeline's brother. After he passed away, in 1873, they bought the farm and moved here from Malone, New York.

In 1890, Laura, Almanzo, and their daughter, Rose, moved to Spring Valley and lived with Almanzo's parents. Their large farmhouse is pictured on page 9. It was a welcome year of rest, since Almanzo and Laura had experienced crop failure, diphtheria, and the loss of their home to a fire.

Construction was started on the Methodist-Episcopal Church in 1876. Almanzo's parents and family were very supportive members. Laura, Almanzo, and Rose attended this church while living in Spring Valley. Today it is a beautiful museum.

The church has Griselle-style windows, imported from England in 1876. This window is over the front door.

Malone, New York - Location for the Book, *Farmer Boy*

Laura never visited the Wilder farm, but wrote *Farmer Boy* from what Almanzo told her. This farm was originally eighty-eight acres and is located along the Trout River. The restored farm home is seen at the right.

Almanzo described the barns in detail. The barns were reconstructed, as seen below, using the drawings he had made for Laura.

A one room school has been added to the area. This is enjoyed by all ages on visits to the farm.

Keystone, South Dakota, Carrie Ingalls' Home for over 35 years

Pa's Hymn Book
Signed by Charles Ingalls, Laura, and Robert Boast

Carrie Ingalls moved to Keystone in 1911, to manage a local newspaper, *Keystone Recorder*.

She married a widower, David Swanzey, on August 1, 1912. Leaving the newspaper business, she devoted her time to raising two stepchildren, Mary (8) and Harry (6).

The Keystone Historical Museum is shown above and has many displays from the 1900 era. There is memorabilia of the Ingalls' family (Pa's Hymn Book is above), as well as many of Carrie's personal items. The museum has information about historic places in the Keystone area and a unique gift shop.

Here are a few of Carrie's personal items, displayed at the museum.

Carrie's Jewelry

Mansfield, Missouri, Where the Little House Books Were Written

See pages 60 - 70 for more pictures of Mansfield

ROCKY RIDGE FARM
HOME OF LAURA INGALLS WILDER

Laura Ingalls Wilder, one of America's best known authors, was born in 1867 near Pepin, Wisconsin. Her "Little House" books were written here on Rocky Ridge Farm, her home for over sixty years.

On July 17, 1894, Laura, her husband Almanzo Wilder, and their seven-year old daughter Rose, left De Smet, South Dakota, in search of a new home. Traveling by covered wagon they arrived in Mansfield on August 30.

On September 24, the Wilders purchased forty acres of land, including the site on which you stand. Here they established Rocky Ridge, a dairy, fruit, and poultry farm. A new house was built and the farm enlarged to nearly two hundred acres.

In 1911, Laura started a career as a journalist, writing about rural life. Between 1932 and 1943, she published the "Little House" books from her memories of pioneer life.

Almanzo died at Rocky Ridge in 1949, at the age of 92. Laura lived here until her death at 90, in 1957.

(Continued on other side)
This marker is the gift of the Missouri State Council of the International Reading Association, the school children of Missouri, their parents and teachers, 1994

People from all over the world enjoy visiting Rocky Ridge Farm and Rock House, where Laura lived and wrote her Little House books.

The museum, pictured below, is enjoyed by every Little House fan. There are many of Laura's family and personal items, including Pa's fiddle. Some of the original manuscript tablets are stored here.

The graves of Almanzo, Laura, and their daughter, Rose Wilder Lane, are at the Mansfield Cemetery.

Independence, Kansas

The Ingalls family lived here from 1869 until 1871. The 1870 census lists them in Rutland Township, Montgomery County. Carrie was born here on August 3, 1870.

Replica Cabin

There is a replica cabin, built at the site in 1977. The furnishings inside the cabin are simple, like those described in *Little House on the Prairie.*

Visitors see Sunny Side School, a one-room schoolhouse built in 1872 and used until 1947.

Sunny Side School and Post Office

A post office (at right in picture) was moved here from nearby Wayside, Kansas. The mailboxes date back to 1885.

An 1880s farmhouse is now the Prairie Gift Store and the office for this museum. It is fun to hike to Walnut Creek, using a footbridge built by the Boy Scouts. Many prairie wildflowers can be seen along the trail.

Iowa Braille and Sight Saving School, Vinton, Iowa

Mary registered in 1881

Iowa Braille and Sight Saving School was founded in 1852. Reverend Alden, a traveling missionary, told the Ingalls family about the school.

The School During Mary's Time

Mary was born in Pepin, Wisconsin, in 1865. In 1881, at the age of sixteen, she enrolled in this school. From the academic records, we can tell that Mary achieved well.

Mary graduated in June, 1889. There were eight in her graduation class. She passed away in 1928, while living with Carrie in Keystone, SD.

The School Today

Herbert Hoover Library, West Branch, Iowa

Herbert Hoover was born in West Branch in 1874 and became 31st President in 1928.

Laura's daughter, Rose, wrote a biography of Herbert Hoover in 1920. Several years after Rose passed away, the library approached Roger Lea MacBride asking for copies of any correspondence between Rose and Hoover. MacBride became acquainted with the Hoover staff and facilities.

Herbert Hoover Library & Museum

Examining Laura's manuscript
The First Four Years

After becoming acquainted with the Hoover Library, he concluded with it would be a good home for the "Rose Wilder Lane Papers." Included with Rose's papers were typed drafts of Laura's Little House books, correspondence between Rose and Laura, correspondence with publishers, and miscellaneous Ingalls family documents. Also in the collection was the manuscript for *The First Four Years,* published by MacBride in 1971.

LAURA INGALLS WILDER FAMILY CHRONOLOGY
1836 - 1881

1836, Jan. 10 Charles Ingalls,(Pa), born in Cuba, NY

1839, Dec. 12 Caroline Lake Quiner,(Ma), born in Milwaukee County, WI

1840 James Wilder family purchases farm near Malone, NY

1857, Feb. 13 Almanzo James Wilder born near Malone, NY

1860 Charles Ingalls & Caroline Quiner marry in Concord, WI

1863, Sept. 23 Charles Ingalls purchases farm in Pepin County, WI

1865, Jan. 10 Mary Amelia Ingalls born in Pepin, WI

1867, Feb. 7 Laura Elizabeth Ingalls born in Pepin, WI

1868 Charles Ingalls sells land in Pepin; buys land in Chariton County, MO

1869 Ingalls leave Chariton County, MO for Montgomery County, KS

1870, Aug. 3 Caroline Celestia (Carrie) Ingalls born in Montgomery County, KS

1871 Ingalls family returns to Pepin, WI; land not paid for and returned to Pa

1871, Oct. Laura starts school at Barry Corner School - 1/2 mile down road

1874 Ingalls family moves to Walnut Grove, MN; buy dugout on Plum Creek

1875 James Wilder family leaves Malone, NY; moves to Spring Valley, MN

1875 Pa built a new house on credit; lost crop to grasshoppers. Pa walks 200 miles to find work. Family moves into town of Walnut Grove

1875 Charles Frederick Ingalls,(Freddie), born in Walnut Grove, MN

1876 Ingalls go to Troy, MN - spend summer with Uncle Pete's family

1876, August 27 - Freddie dies

1876, Fall Ingalls move to Burr Oak, IA help Steadmans manage Masters Hotel

1877, May 23 Grace Pearl Ingalls born in Burr Oak, IA

1878, Jan. Ingalls move back to Walnut Grove; live with Ensign Family for winter; rejoin Congregational Church

1879 Mary becomes blind; Ingalls family moves to De Smet, SD

1880 Pa files Homestead Claim

1881 Hard winter; Ingalls move to town; twist hay to burn

1881, Fall Mary enrolls in Iowa Braille and Sight Saving School, Vinton, IA

LAURA INGALLS WILDER FAMILY CHRONOLOGY
1882 - 1971

1882 Laura gets first teaching job Bouchie School, earns $20/month; 12 miles south of De Smet

1884 Laura teaches at Perry School for $25/month; Laura Ingalls and Almanzo Wilder engaged

1885 Aug. 25 Laura and Almanzo married by Rev. Brown, in De Smet, SD

1886, Dec. 5-Rose Wilder born in De Smet

1887 Pa & Ma Ingalls move into town of De Smet, SD (on Third Street)

1888 winter - Laura & Almanzo have diphtheria

1889 Aug. Infant son of Laura and Almanzo dies; home lost to a fire

1890, May Laura, Almanzo, & Rose move to Spring Valley, MN; live with Wilder family

1891 Laura, Almanzo, & Rose take train to Florida

1892 They return to De Smet, SD

1894, July; Wilders leave for Missouri

1894, Aug. 31 They reach Mansfield, MO

1894, Sept. 24 Wilders buy Rocky Ridge Farm

1898 Manly, Laura, & Rose move to town; rent house for $5/mo; Rent out farm home

1902 Charles Ingalls, (Pa), dies

1903 Rose goes with Aunt Eliza Jane to Crowley, LA

1904 Rose graduates from Crowley H. S.

1909 Rose & Gillette Lane marry

1911 Laura's first published article appears in Missouri Ruralist

1918 Rose and Gillette divorce

1919 Laura writes for McCalls Magazine with Rose

1924 Caroline Ingalls, (Ma), dies

1928 Rose gives Laura and Almanzo key to Rock House as a Christmas gift

Publication of Little House Books
1932 Little House in the Big Woods
1933 Farmer Boy
1935 Little House on the Prairie
1937 On the Banks of Plum Creek
1939 By the Shores of Silver Lake
1940 The Long Winter
1941 Little Town on the Prairie
1943 These Happy Golden Years

1949 Almanzo Wilder dies

1954 L. I. Wilder Award established

1957 Laura dies
1962 On the Way Home-publ. by Rose
1968 Rose Lane dies
1971 First Four Years publ by R. MacBride

CREDITS

All photos in this book are by the authors, with these exceptions. We are grateful for permission to use the following

6   newspaper announcements
LIW Memorial Society, De Smet, SD

7   wedding photo
Courtesy of Laura Ingalls Wilder Home Association, Mansfield, MO

8-9 newspaper announcements
LIW Memorial Society, De Smet, SD

9   Wilder Farm Home
Spring Valley Historical Society, Spring Valley, MN

11-12 historic pictures and newspaper ad
LIW Memorial Society, De Smet, SD

15-16 Burbank Cottage and ferry picture (historic photo)
Dakota Territorial Museum, Yankton, SD

16 pontoon bridge
South Dakota State Historical Society, Pierre, SD

25 Chautauqua Park
Gage County Historical Society, Beatrice, NE

34,36,37 historical photos
Kansas State Historical Society, Topeka, KS

39 Mural
Clinton Lake Corps of Engineers Visitor Center, Artist Randall Bennett

51-52 Historic photos
Barton County Historical Society, Lamar, MO

56 Historic photos
History Museum for Springfield-Greene County, Springfield, MO

57,59 (from 1889)
Springfield-Greene County Library, Springfield, MO

60 Mansfield Bank (historic photo)   61 Church & Carnival (historic photo)
Mansfield Historical Society, Mansfield, MO

62 Town Square (historic photo)   63 Holiday Parade (historic photo)
Mansfield Historical Society, Mansfield, MO

65, 66, 67, 69 Wilder Family Photos
Courtesy of Laura Ingalls Wilder Home Association, Mansfield, MO

77 Historic Photo - Iowa Braille and Sight Saving School